CLASSIC PIANO REPERTOIRE
LYNN FREEMAN OLSON

13 DISTINCTIVE PIANO SOLOS

CONTENTS

ISBN 978-1-5400-5402-9

WILLIS MUSIC

EXCLUSIVELY DISTRIBUTED BY

HAL•LEONARD®

© 2019 by The Willis Music Co.
International Copyright Secured   All Rights Reserved

Visit Hal Leonard Online at
www.halleonard.com

Contact us:
Hal Leonard
7777 West Bluemound Road
Milwaukee, WI 53213
Email: info@halleonard.com

In Europe, contact:
Hal Leonard Europe Limited
42 Wigmore Street
Marylebone, London, W1U 2RN
Email: info@halleonardeurope.com

In Australia, contact:
Hal Leonard Australia Pty. Ltd.
4 Lentara Court
Cheltenham, Victoria, 3192 Australia
Email: info@halleonard.com.au

FROM THE PUBLISHERS

The *Classic Piano Repertoire* series includes popular as well as lesser-known pieces from a select group of composers out of the Willis piano archives. This volume features 13 distinctive piano works by Lynn Freeman Olson, progressing from early to mid-intermediate. Each piece has been newly engraved and edited with the aim to preserve Olson's original intent and musical purpose.

It was William Gillock who encouraged Willis Music to publish Olson's works posthumously in the early 1990s. Gillock spent his own final years carefully editing and revising his friend's unpublished works with the permission of the Lynn Freeman Olson Estate. Many of the pieces are included in these new compilations.

From the article "Pianist is in tune with students" featuring **LYNN FREEMAN OLSON**:

> Seated before the piano, [Olson] played separate sections of a sonatina and compared the melodies to people. "This is a story happening, like *Dynasty*," he said. Landing on a short series of chords, "Here's the crowd, they have something to report..." "Here's the soprano again, she's so nervous," he said, playing a few quick notes in the upper line.
>
> "That's overdoing it," he said upon finishing. "But I really feel it is like a story... (and if) music isn't this exciting, we shouldn't be teaching it."

> — Jennifer Strobel
> *The Free Lance-Star;* May 2, 1985

LYNN FREEMAN OLSON (1938-1987) was born and raised in Minneapolis, Minnesota. He received degrees in piano performance and pedagogy from the University of Minnesota and later studied with Frances Clark, founder of the New School for Music Study. Olson was incredibly prolific in his short life, composing over 1200 works for piano alone, in addition to children's songs, choral works, and music for theater and radio. Olson also contributed music to the *Captain Kangaroo Show* on CBS. He continues to be remembered today for his distinctive composition style, often incorporating unusual harmonies and meters not generally found in early teaching music.

Olson spent most of his adult life in New York City, where he died in 1987 at the age of 49.

Italian Street Singer

Lynn Freeman Olson

Strolling tempo; songlike

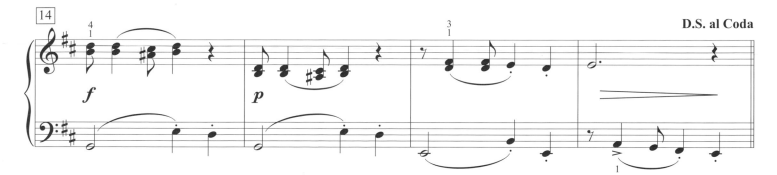

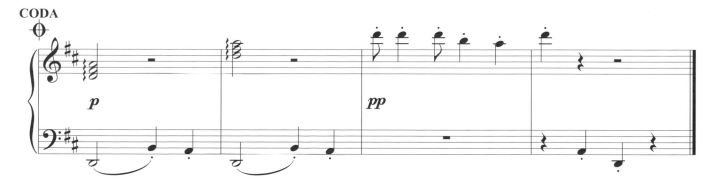

Whirlwind

Lynn Freeman Olson

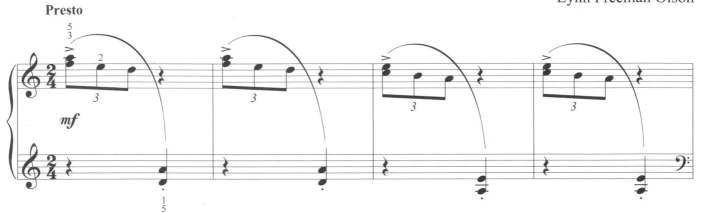

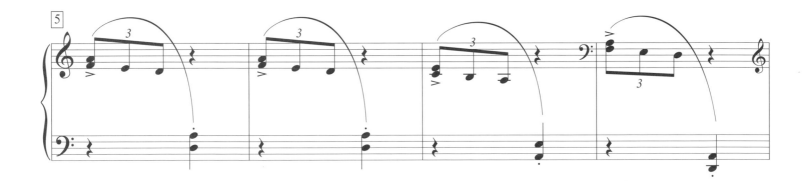

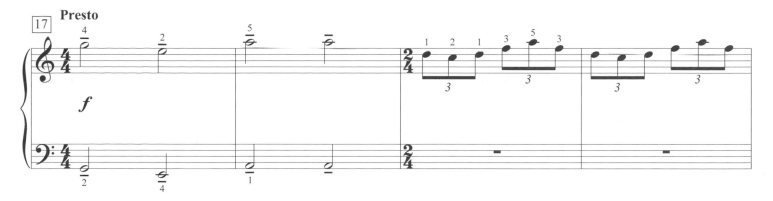

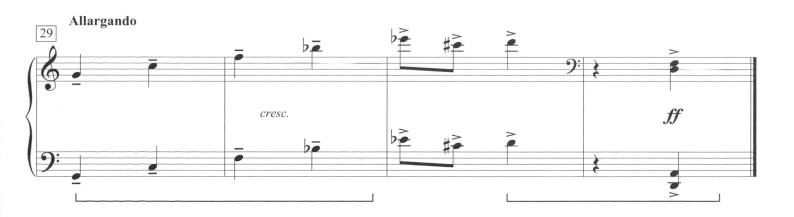

The Flying Ship

Lynn Freeman Olson

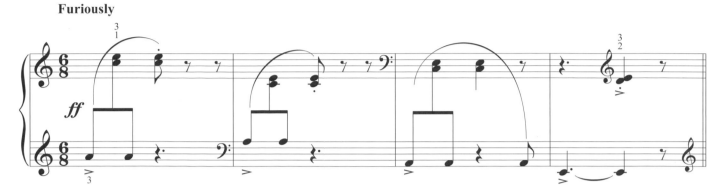

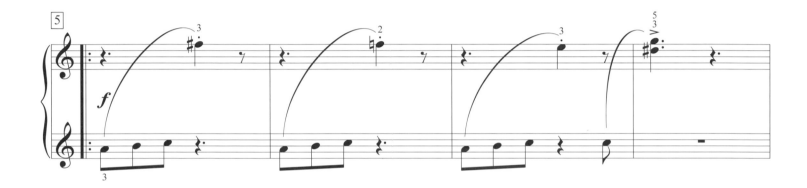

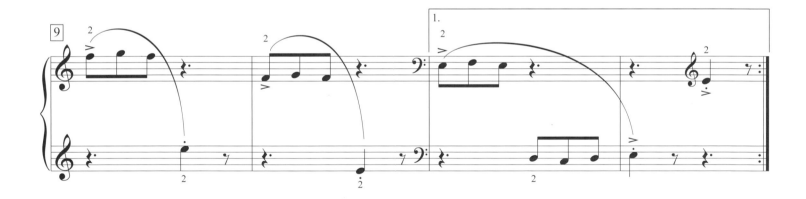

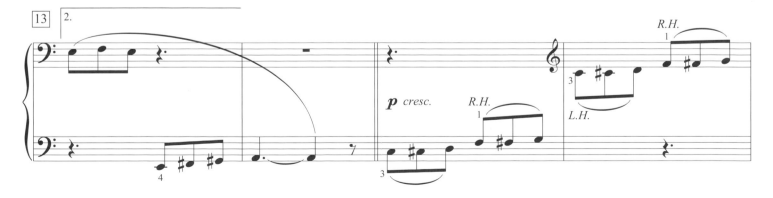

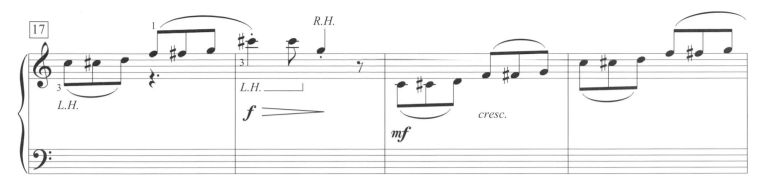

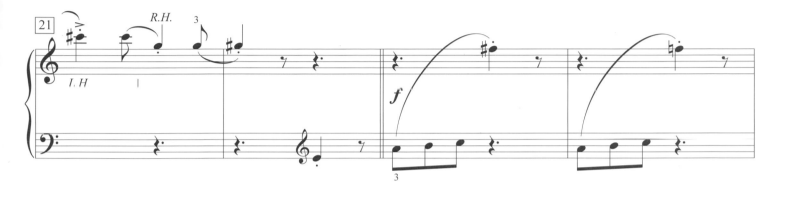

Cloud Paintings

Lynn Freeman Olson

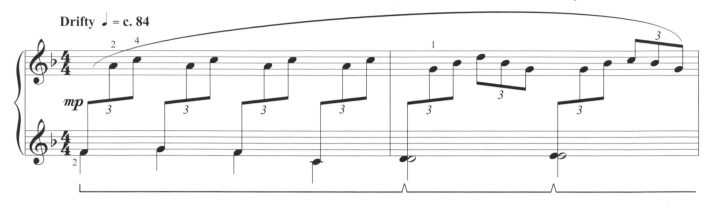

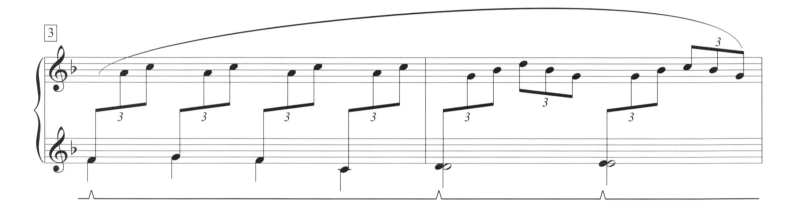

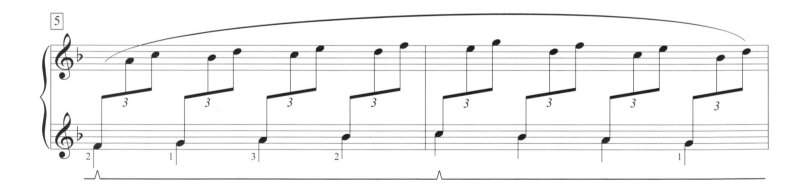

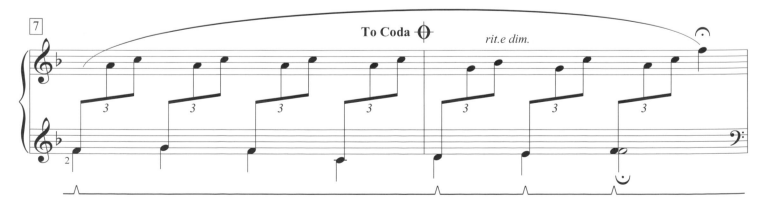

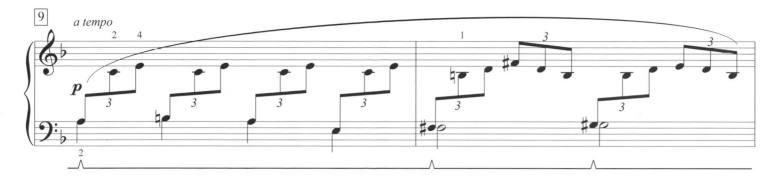

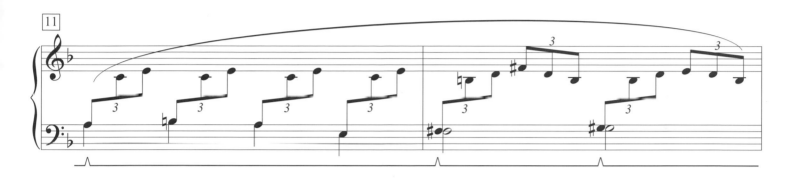

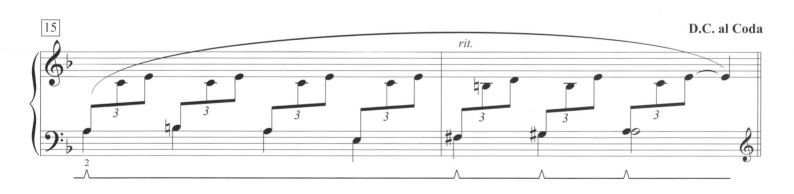

Theme and Variations

Lynn Freeman Olson

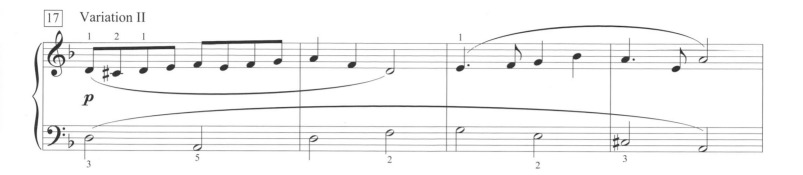

17 Variation II

21

25 Theme

29

33 Codetta

Pageant Dance

Lynn Freeman Olson

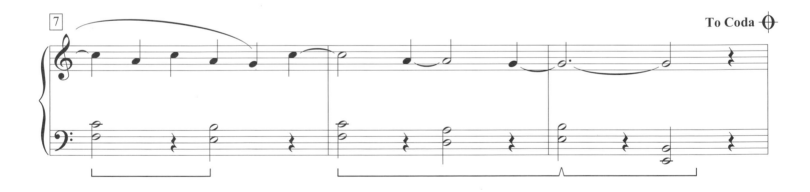

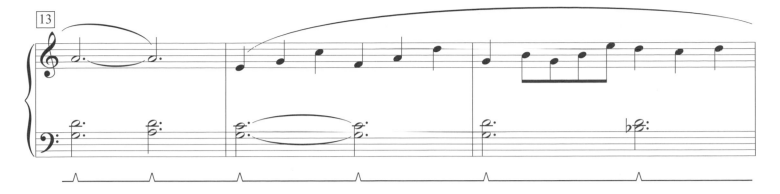

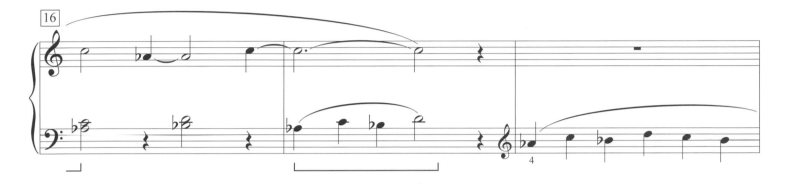

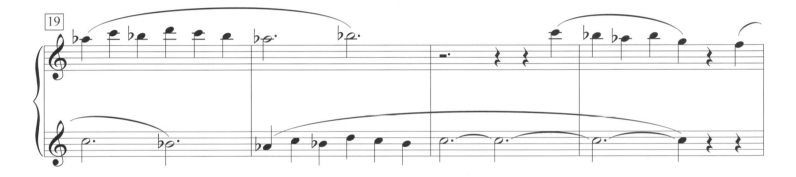

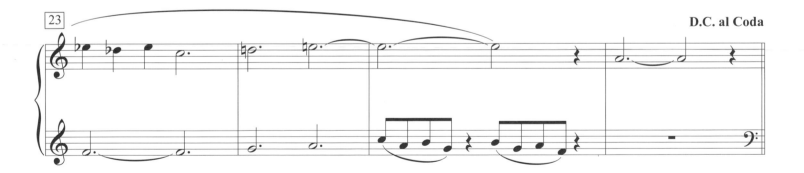

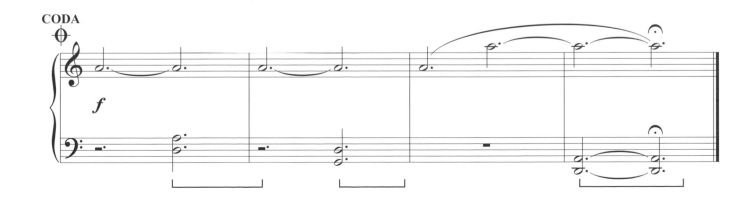

"In Fourteen Hundred Ninety-Two..."

Lynn Freeman Olson

Brisk March tempo ♩ = 76 - 84

Setting sail!

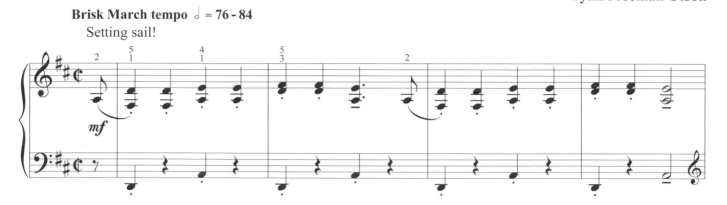

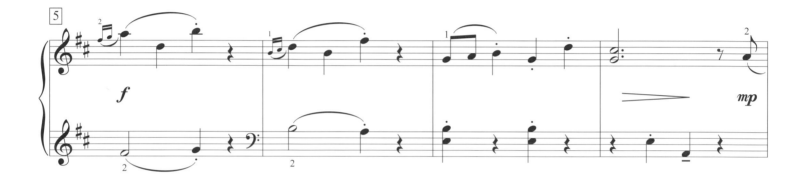

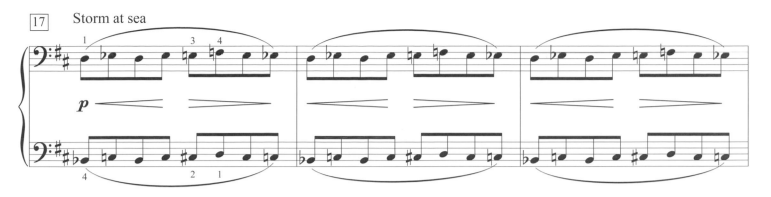

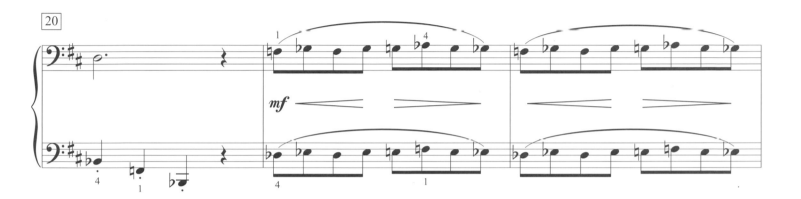

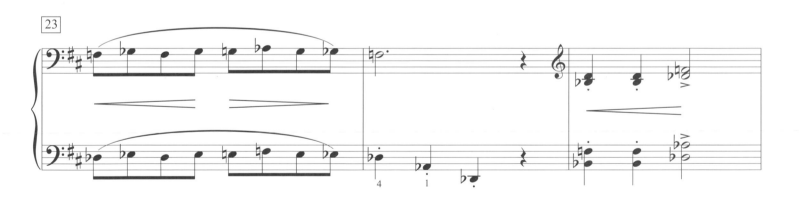

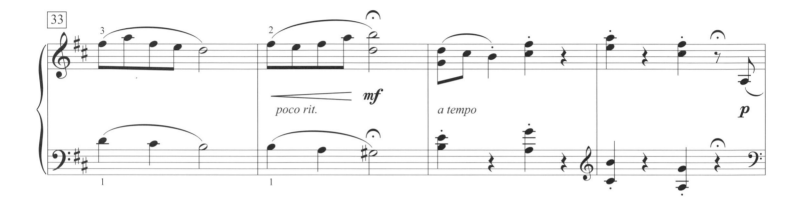

Mexican Serenade

Lynn Freeman Olson

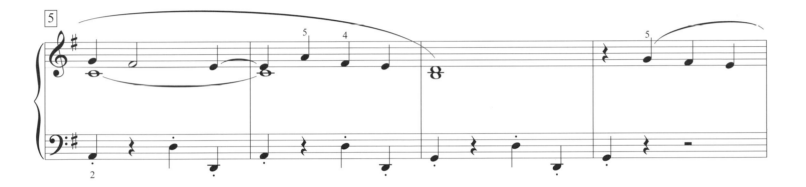

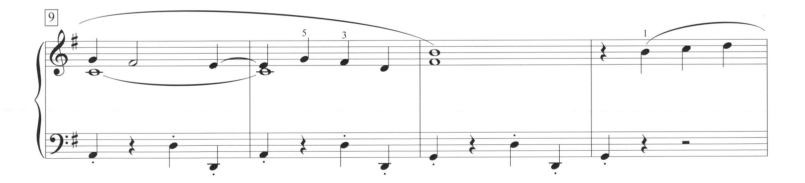

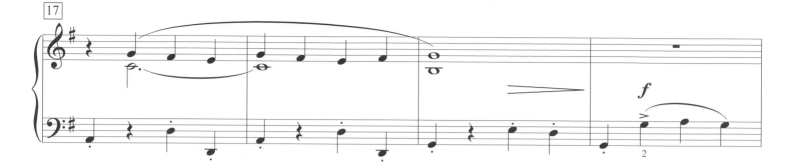

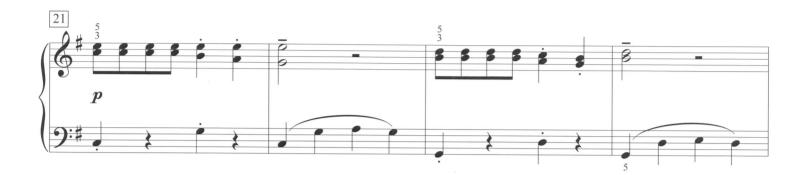

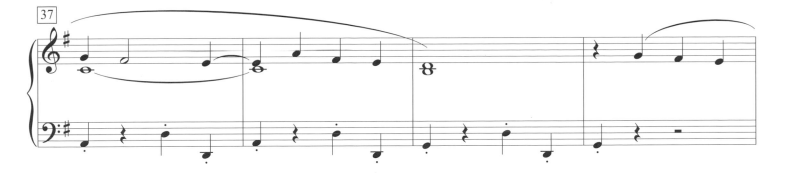

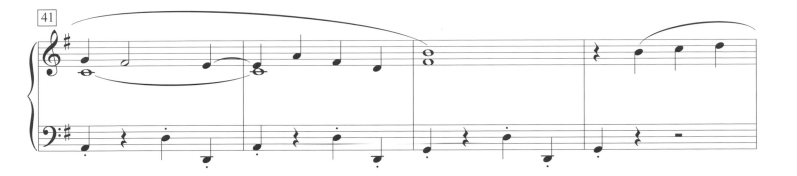

Rather Blue

Lynn Freeman Olson

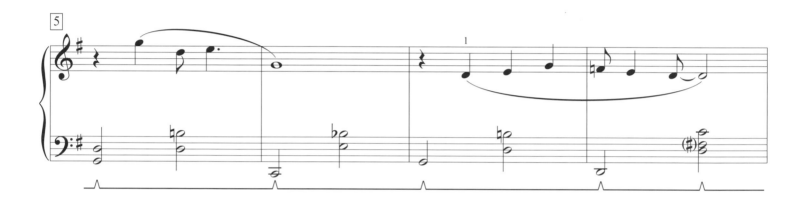

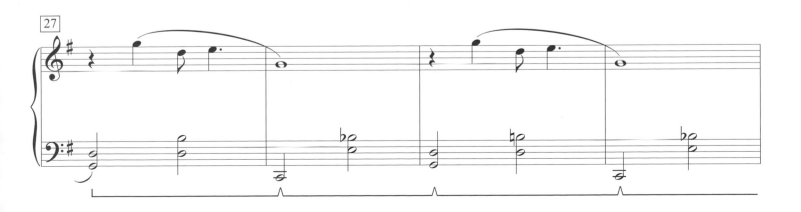

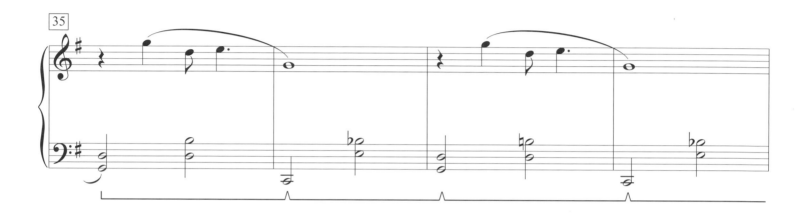

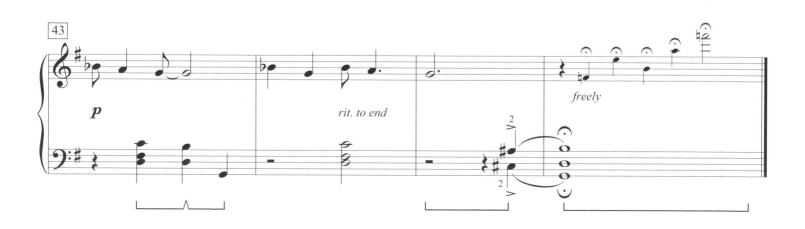

Brazilian Holiday

Lynn Freeman Olson

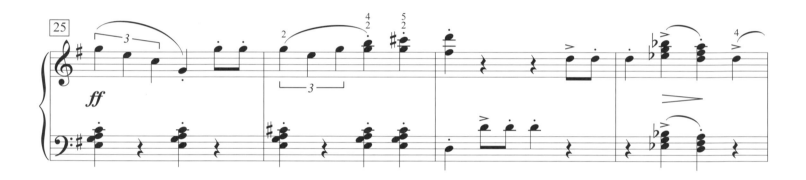

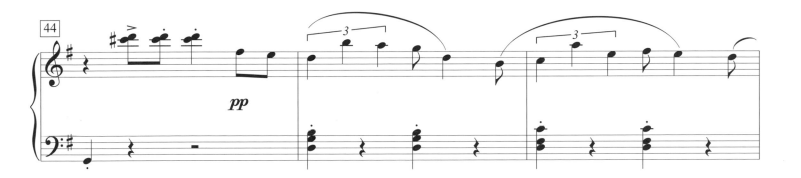

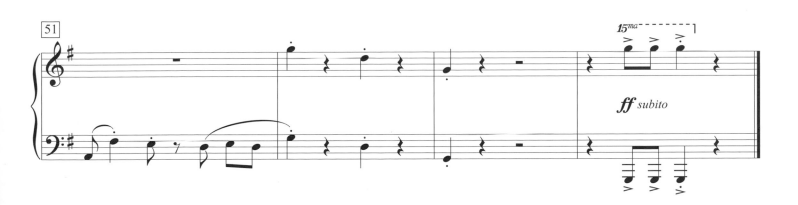

Heroic Event

Lynn Freeman Olson

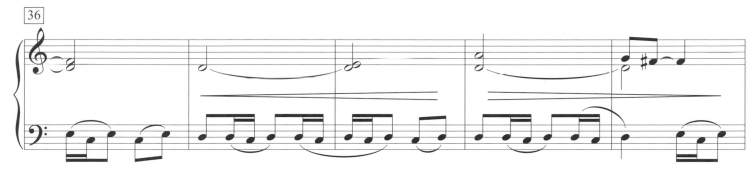

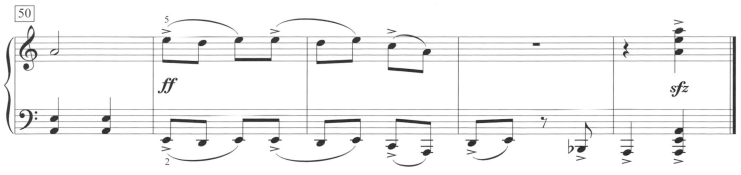

Fanfare

Lynn Freeman Olson

Very fast; detached

Use fingers 1 and 5 in both hands throughout

To Frances Clark
Lynn delighted in Frances Clark's warm and hearty laugh in response to humorous music.
In "Band Wagon," it is that laugh he is reaching for!

Band Wagon

Lynn Freeman Olson

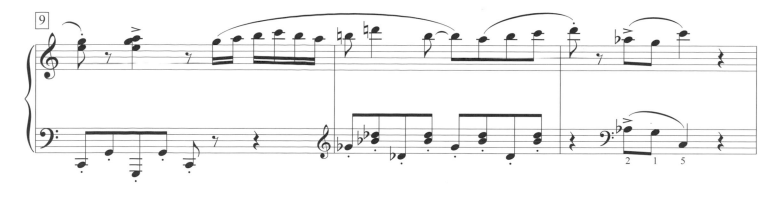

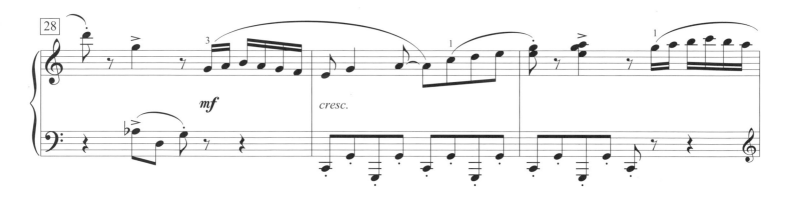

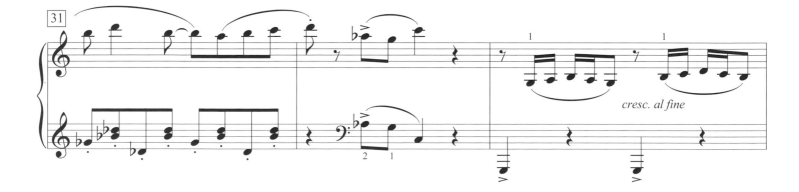

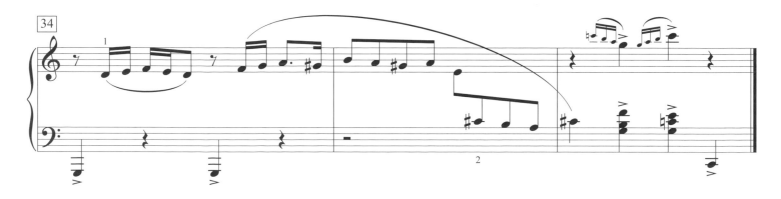